I0151909

# Mentoring For Marriage

*A Seven-Week*
*Interactive Course Designed*
*to Prepare Couples for Marriage*

**Daryl G. Donovan**

CSS Publishing Company, Inc.
Lima, Ohio

MENTORING FOR MARRIAGE

Copyright © 2014 by
CSS Publishing Company, Inc.
Lima, Ohio

All rights reserved. No part of this publication may be reproduced in any manner whatsoever without the prior permission of the publisher, except in the case of brief quotations embodied in critical articles and reviews. Inquiries should be addressed to: Permissions, CSS Publishing Company, Inc., 5450 N. Dixie Highway, Lima, Ohio 45807.

Scripture quotations are from the New American Standard Bible, © 1960, 1962, 1963, 1968, 1971, 1972, 1973, 1975, 1977 by The Lockman Foundation. Used by permission.

**Library of Congress Cataloging-in-Publication Data**

Donovan, Daryl G.
      Mentoring for marriage : a seven-week interactive course designed to prepare couples for marriage / Daryl G. Donovan.
          pages  cm
      ISBN 0-7880-2803-0  (alk. paper)
      1. Marriage--Religious aspects--Christianity--Study and teaching. 2. Marriage mentoring--Study and teaching. 3. Marriage counseling--Study and teaching. I. Title.

      BV835.D66   2014
      259'.13--dc23

                                                    2014019870

For more information about CSS Publishing Company resources, visit our website at www.csspub.com, email us at csr@csspub.com, or call (800) 241-4056.

electronic file:
ISBN-13: 978-0-7880-2804-5
ISBN-10: 0-7880-2804-9


ISBN-13: 978-0-7880-2803-8
ISBN-10: 0-7880-2803-0                              PRINTED IN USA

# Table of Contents

# Introduction

*"For this cause a man shall leave his father and mother and shall leave to his wife and the two shall become one flesh."*
(Ephesians 5:31)

In the very next verse in Ephesians, Paul refers to marriage as a mystery. Marriage is a wonderfully supernatural act of God making a man and woman one.

The two of you are about to embark upon an exciting life adventure that will profoundly change everything about your life.

The Bible is full of practical counsel to enable you to experience marriage at its best. For seven sessions you will look intently into the word of God, and into each other's hearts, allowing God to prepare you for the mystery of marriage.

# A Message to Pastors

Pre-marital counseling is an essential ingredient for a successful marriage. It requires a commitment on the part of the pastor, the couple, and the church to see to it that effective preparation for marriage is done. *Mentoring For Marriage* is an interactive tool designed to not only prepare a couple for marriage but to build relationships between the pastor and the couple, and if desired, with a mentoring couple in your congregation.

The seven sessions presented in this workbook can be conducted by the pastor or by a trusted, mature mentoring couple. As the pastor, you will need to meet with potential mentoring couples, review the material, and discern if they feel adequate for the task and are qualified.

As pastor, if you choose to work through a mentoring couple, you will probably want to meet with the couple to be married once at the beginning to do some marriage planning and present the pre-marital counseling plan, and at the conclusion of the counseling sessions to review how things have progressed.

*Mentoring For Marriage* is not designed to tell a couple everything they need in preparation for marriage. It is designed to get couples talking about significant issues they will face as husband and wife, and encourage them to pursue that dialogue.

Marriage is a great adventure… and *Mentoring For Marriage* will help couples be better prepared to launch out on that adventure.

# A Word
# to the Mentoring Couple

You have been entrusted with a tremendous, rewarding opportunity to mentor a couple preparing for marriage. As you pledge to meet with them during these seven sessions, be open about your own marriage, sharing the wisdom you have learned from your successes and failures.

Listen carefully to the young couple. Sometimes a question aptly put, with attentiveness to the response, is far more valuable than many words.

While *Mentoring For Marriage* is a very basic course, it is designed to get to the key issues of marriage. While it is acceptable to pursue other topics, be certain to cover the course work prescribed.

In the event that problem areas do surface as you proceed through the course, do not hesitate to include your pastor or a Christian counselor in the process.

Have a great seven sessions as you help to prepare this couple for a wonderful life relationship.

# Course Guidelines
# for the Mentoring Couple

1. While this course can work in a formal setting, such as the church building, it is best to have the couple come to your home. You may even want to meet at a restaurant.

2. Build a relationship with the couple. Have them over to eat with you. Pray for them and with them regularly. Talk about other issues of life as you get to know them.

3. Do not read the material to them when you are together (unless you think they haven't). They are supposed to complete the unit and answer all questions. Discuss their responses together.

4. Become familiar with the material in *Mentoring For Marriage*. Other helpful resources are suggested, which you might want to have on hand.

5. Don't go more than ninety minutes. One hour should be adequate for the course material with thirty minutes for fellowship and prayer.

6. Keep your pastor updated as to the progress of the pre-marital sessions.

7. Always begin and end with prayer.

# Mentoring Couple's Guide

**Session 1**
**How Do You Know This Is The One?**
• Begin your time together with prayer.
• After you have asked them how they met, tell them how you met your husband/wife.
• Proceed through all of the questions of the session, allowing both to respond. Feel free to jot down notes of their responses in your material.
• If the couple is sexually active and does not plan to discontinue that activity, you must inform them that they must look elsewhere for counsel and marriage unless the marrying pastor has given other directions.
• Close with prayer.

**Session 2**
**Pulling Together With Christ**
• Begin your time together with prayer.
• Go through the assigned material with them, allowing them both to respond.
• If you discover that one, or both of them are not Christians, you will need to address that issue. This could be a good opportunity to present God's plan of salvation.[1]
• Close with prayer.

**Session 3**
**One + One = One**
• Begin with prayer.
• Go through the material giving each of them an opportunity to share.
• At some point share your own experience of oneness in your marriage.
• Close with prayer. Pray specifically if there is an area of concern regarding oneness.

## Session 4
## The Unique Assignment
• Begin your time together with prayer.
• Review their responses to the questions in the material.
• Each of you share about your role in your marriage.
  - Share how your wife has been a "helper" to you.
  - Share how your husband has loved you sacrificially.
• Pray with the couple as you close.


## Session 5
## Financial Feuds Can Fuel Failure
• Pray as you begin your time together.
• Compare the couple's responses to the questions on page 53.
• Discuss areas of concern.
• Share your own budget experiences. Crown Financial Ministries is a great resource here (www.crown.org).
• Review the responses of each to the questions in the remainder of the unit.
• Close with prayer.


## Session 6
## My Body Is Not My Own
• Pray as you begin.
• While sex is a delicate topic to discuss, it is important to be as candid, yet sensitive as possible. The couple needs to be encouraged that it is acceptable to discuss sexual issues.[2]
• Review the responses each has written to the material in the unit.
• You may want to pursue further how men and women approach sex differently. You may even want to have some "woman to woman" and "man to man" time on this topic.
• Close your session with prayer.

**Session 7**
**The 3-D/3-C Marriage**
• Begin with prayer.
• Review the responses each has written in the unit.
• Talk about how important the 3 C's have been in your own marriage.
- Christ
- Communication
- Commitment
• If either has been divorced, take the time to review the questions on page 81.
• Have a closure celebration with the couple as this is their final session. Present them with a Certificate of Completion.
• Pray a blessing on this couple. Pray that their wedding day be a powerful tribute to God's gift of marriage and may it bring glory to Jesus Christ!

---

1. An excellent tool for presenting the gospel is a booklet subtitled "Why Jesus?" written by Nicky Gumble, available through David C. Cook.

2. An excellent resource for this session would be Dr. Ed Wheat's book, *Intended for Pleasure*.

# Session 1

# How Do You
# Know This Is The One?

# How Do You Know This Is The One?

**Tell about how you met your fiancé/fiancée.**

**What was it that attracted you to your fiancé/fiancée?**

## 1. Considering God's Counsel

> *"So the men of Israel took some of their provisions, and did not ask for the counsel of the Lord. Joshua made peace with them and made a covenant with them, to let them live; and the leaders of the congregation swore an oath to them."*
> (Joshua 9:14-15)

Israel entered into a covenant with the Gibeonites. This covenant proved to be a horrible snare for them. If only they had sought the counsel of God, they would have never found themselves in this painful dilemma.

Marriage is a covenant relationship. The word *covenant* means to make an unbreakable promise. The wedding ring itself is a symbol of the marriage covenant. It is an unbroken circle, signifying an unbreakable lifelong commitment. Covenant-making is a critical time to seek the counsel of God.

**Tell about how you have asked for God's counsel in your relationship.**

When my fiancée and I went to our pre-marital counseling, the pastor said, "I have only one question to ask you. Are you confident that God brought you together to be married?" We both answered "Yes."

The most important matter in your relationship is whether you have clearly received the counsel of God that you are to enter into this lifelong covenant. One of the reasons half of marriages end in divorce is that couples have not made the effort to clearly discern the will of God for their relationship. Was it really God who brought you together? Are you certain He brought you together to be married?

**Are you confident that God brought you together to be married?**

_____ yes          _____ no          _____ unsure

**Explain your response.**

## 2. How Do You Know?

*He said, "O Lord, the God of my master Abraham, please grant me success today, and show lovingkindness to my master Abraham. Behold I am standing by the spring, and the daughters of the men of the city are coming out to draw water; now may it be that the girl to whom I say, 'Please let down your jar so that I may drink,' and who answers, 'Drink, and I will water your camels also'; may she be the one whom thou hast appointed for your servant Isaac; and by this I will know that you have shown lovingkindness to my master."*
(Genesis 24:12-14)

Abraham sent Eliezer off on a "wife hunt." His assignment was to find God's woman for Abraham's son, Isaac. With an unusual prayer, Eliezer asked for the counsel of God and a clear confirmation of Miss Right. As soon as Eliezer finished his prayer, Rebekah walked up, gave him a drink, then offered to water the camels also. God had given his counsel.

Discerning who you are to marry will probably not involve a herd of camels. Nevertheless, God does want to give you his counsel. How does a couple clearly capture the heart and will of God for their relationship?

a. Eliezer prayed. Prayer is the starting place for knowing the will of God. When you pray be certain you are *asking* God for his will, not *telling* God what you think his will should be.

**Tell about how you have prayed concerning your relationship, and what you have discerned through prayer.**

b. Eliezer had orders from his master that set certain requirements and standards for the marriage partner of Isaac. We also have clear directives in God's word that provide marriage guidelines for us. The Bible is a great source of God's counsel.

The Bible, for example, makes it very clear that a Christian is not to marry a non-Christian (so many ignore that counsel). Second Corinthians 6:14 says, "Do not be bound together with unbelievers."

Be certain your relationship lines up with the biblical standard. If you have any question as to whether it does or not, talk with your pastor, counselor, or mentor for clarification.

**To what degree are you confident that your relationship lines up with God's will as reflected in the Bible?**
0      1      2      3      4      5      6      7      8      9      10

**Explain.**

c. God's will was confirmed by family and others. When Eliezer explained to Rebekah's father the way God had led him, Laban replied, "The matter comes from the Lord."

Has your relationship been confirmed by others who know you and love you? If you do not have the blessing of your parents for this marriage, that does *not* necessarily mean you are out of God's will. It does mean, however, that you must consider your ways carefully and seek wise counsel from trusted Christian leadership as you proceed.

The counsel of your pastor is another important confirmation of your relationship. Ask your pastor to be in prayer with you and seek a candid appraisal from your pastor regarding your marriage.

**List those who have confirmed that they see the pleasure of God in your union, such as your pastor, parents, and friends.**

**List those who have expressed concern about your marriage.**

### 3. A Matter of the Heart

Marriage is a gift from God. He has brought you together because you will find greater joy in life together than you ever could alone. He has also brought you together because you can more fully fulfill your life-purpose married to the one he has brought to you than you could alone.

When considering God's will for marriage, at the core of the matter is the heart. What is it that motivates you to be joined to a life-mate? The motivation to please God and serve God more fully must be a central consideration.

Simply said, will this union make you more effective for Christ? Has that question been a part of your consideration as you have tried to know God's will?

\* \* \*

God called me to be a pastor when I was seventeen. At that time I was dating a girl who was not a Christian. When I shared with her that God had called me to be a pastor, she was angry. With deep emotion she said, "I'll never be a pastor's wife! You've got to decide now! It's this 'call' of yours — or it's me!" That was one of the hardest decisions of my life. I was at one of those life-decision crossroads. After several days of agonizing prayer, I was able to gently tell her that I must be faithful to the call.

* * *

It is very clear from the example that the relationship I was in was not one that would enhance my ability to serve God. Not every relationship has that dramatic of a distinction. I do believe, however, if you will earnestly pray and reflect, you will know if the relationship you are in will enable you to more fully accomplish God's purposes in your life.

**How confident are you that your relationship will make you more effective for Christ?**
0     1     2     3     4     5     6     7     8     9     10

**Explain.**

## 4. Sex Clouds the Waters

Have you and your fiancé/fiancée been sexually involved? I am convinced that nothing clouds the will of God more for a couple than pre-marital sex. Josh McDowell once said that couples who are sexually involved are led more by their hormones than by the Holy Spirit.

Since pre-marital sex is clearly out of the will of God, then discerning the will of God for all other matters in the relationship becomes more difficult. If you cannot refrain from sexual involvement prior to the marriage union, there is a strong possibility you are in "lust" rather than in "love."

* * *

Talk with your marriage mentor about the physical aspect of your relationship. If you have already become sexually active, admit it, seek God's forgiveness, and start anew today. First John 1:9 says, "If you confess your sin God is faithful and just and will forgive your sin and cleanse you of all unrighteousness."

**Are you committed to sexual purity throughout your engagement?**

___ yes    ___ no

**Explain.**

## 5. Be Willing to Call Off the Engagement

There are couples who have had caution flags come up at every turn of the relationship, who have received counsel to avoid marriage, yet because of stubbornness or even pride they have gone through with their wedding plans. Unfortunately, those couples have discovered the hard way that their union was not God's desire. While many are divorced, others are in a miserable marriage with regrets for ignoring godly counsel.

As you proceed through your own pre-marital preparation be willing to hear God say "wait" or even "no" to your marriage. It is far better to prevent a serious life mistake than to suffer painful consequences down the road.

**If you discover serious reservations regarding your marriage, to what degree are you willing to wait — or even call off the marriage?**

0    1    2    3    4    5    6    7    8    9    10
not                        maybe                        willing

**Explain.**

**Pray Together:** Ask God to guide you as you prepare for marriage. Ask him to help you be open to fully know his heart and will for you.

# Session 2

# Pulling Together
# With Christ

# Pulling Together With Christ

*"Do not be bound together with unbelievers; for what partnerships have righteousness and lawlessness, or what fellowship has light with darkness?"*
(2 Corinthians 6:14)

**Are you a committed Christian with a personal relationship with Jesus Christ?**

_____ yes _____ no

**Explain.**

**Is your fiancé/fiancée a committed Christian with a personal relationship with Jesus Christ?**

_____ yes _____ no

**Explain.**

**Have you discussed spiritual matters together?**
_____ none _____ a little _____ some _____ often _____ at length

**Explain.**

**Are you in full agreement about spiritual matters?**
_____ I think so _____ yes _____ no _____ I don't know

**Explain.**

\* \* \*

Bill and Sarah had dated in high school. Many regarded them to be the perfect couple. Both had a distant relationship with God. Spiritual matters were not important to either of them.

After high school Bill proposed to Sarah and she accepted an engagement ring from him. During the engagement Sarah had a dramatic encounter with Christ that changed her life. She began attending church services but Bill had no interest. When Sarah would desire to pray together, Bill would refuse.

Sarah received counsel to be careful as she proceeded in the relationship. She believed she could eventually convince Bill to become a Christian. The counselor shared God's word of warning to not be "yoked" to an unbeliever. Even though Bill did not accept Christ, Sarah proceeded with the wedding.

Many years have passed and both Bill and Sarah are unhappy. Their children are confused about spiritual matters, seeing a divided Dad and Mom. Sarah continues to pray for Bill and loves him deeply; however, she knows that the relationship falls short of God's best.

* * *

**List reasons why the Bible discourages the marriage of a believer and a non-believer.**

## 1. This Yoke Is No Joke

"To avoid being bound to an unbeliever" is one of God's strongest warnings. The word "bound" is sometimes translated "yoked." It is a picture of two oxen being yoked together, pulling together to accomplish some task. If one oxen is stronger — or if one is a donkey or a cow, the labor will be more difficult or even impossible. It could actually mean going in frustrating circles, accomplishing nothing.

Don't think that you will convert your spouse after marriage. It is best to enter into marriage with the assumption that "what you see is what you get." While there are cases of post-marriage conversions that led to "happily-ever-after" marriages, please understand those are the exception.

It is also worthy of consideration that just because you are both Christians may not mean you are equally yoked. Often both the man and the woman are Christians but they are not in full agreement on many important spiritual matters. Denominational differences have been a hindrance to some couples. Some have chosen to have "his" church and "her" church. While a couple can grow and have a good relationship without full spiritual agreement, the most desirable situation is one in which they walk in real unity.

**List any spiritual differences you know you have as a couple.**

**Pray about your spiritual differences.**

## 2. Why Is Pulling Together Essential?

Why is it so important for a couple to be "one" when it comes to spiritual matters? Why does the "yoke" need to be equal?

**a. There will be agreement on priorities.**
If church membership and attendance is important to the husband and not to the wife, there will be strife. If Bible reading and prayer are a priority to the wife and not to the husband, the couple will not be pulling together in the same strength and purpose. Nurturing children in the Christian faith must receive equal emphasis from the father and the mother.

When a couple is yoked equally together, spiritually they will discover great unity in the setting of priorities and establishing values. If they are not in unity, values and priorities will always be a source of contention.

* * *

Mack and Sarah both were Christians. They were in agreement on church involvement, but far apart when it came to the issue of money. Sarah believed they should tithe the full 10%. Mack thought

$10 per week was sufficient. Sarah wanted to support an orphaned child in India as well as some missionaries in Russia. Mack wanted to buy a motor home and jet ski so the family could enjoy travel and recreation. The division over these spiritually-related financial priorities kept them constantly at odds.

* * *

Spiritual unity is reflected in a unity of priorities and values.

**To what degree are you in agreement on priorities and values? (Rate 1 to 10, 10 being most)**

0    1    2    3    4    5    6    7    8    9    10

**Explain your response.**

**b. A couple equally yoked can persevere hard times.**
Difficult times will come in every marriage. If a couple shares the same faith foundation, they will share a strength that will sustain them through the storms of life.

The word "persevere" comes from the combination of two words: purpose and severity. When a couple is in unity on the primary purposes of life, based on solid biblical principles, they will be able to endure the severe times of life.

**Do you share a united faith that will see you through the hard times?**

_____ yes      _____ no

**Explain your answer.**

**c. A third product of spiritual unity in a marriage is pleasure.**
You will have great joy in your relationship because you share common faith. Conflicts can be brought to resolution when Christ is at the center of the relationship to help you.

As we will discuss in another unit, the saying is true that "the family who prays together stays together." Not only do they stay together, they enjoy being together.

The marriage relationship is to be one of fulfillment and delight. It is only when there is the sense of a common spiritual yoke that couples can enjoy the reality of a fulfilling marriage.

I probably shouldn't say this, but I always tell couples prior to marriage, "Over 50% of couples who stand at the altar like you, will soon end up divorcing. Of the 50% of those who stay married, 50% of them are miserable." You've seen couples who are enduring marriage. While I commend their commitment, I grieve because they are missing the pleasure God intended for them. Other than our relationship with Christ, the marriage relationship is to be the most significant, life-giving relationship we will experience on this planet! The greatest pleasure will come as the yoke is equal and the couple pulls firmly together in the strength of Christ Jesus, led by the Spirit of God in the same direction.

**What are some other benefits being equally yoked can bring to your marriage?**


### 3. What if We Are Equally Yoked as Unbelievers?

The warning in scripture is to refrain from uniting a believer to a non-believer. Is it okay for two non-believers to marry?

While there is no restriction pertaining to the marriage of two non-believers, there is a reason the scripture is silent on the matter. Typically non-believers are not going to seek the counsel of God's word. The Bible is primarily addressed to believers to tell us God's will.

Why would unbelievers want a church wedding anyway? For some a church wedding is merely a matter of custom rather than faith.

People get married in churches. It's beautiful to get married in a church. While most couples want the blessing of God on their union, some don't genuinely desire the will of God for their lives.

If marriage is being done primarily to fulfill a legal requirement or because of custom, a justice of the peace in a non-church situation would be more appropriate for non-believers.

## In Conclusion

The picture of an oxen yoke is a great illustration of marital teamwork. You must be pulling in the same direction with equal strength. That direction must be led by the Holy Spirit and the strength must come from the Lord.

**Are you both pulling in the same direction and relying on God's strength?**

_____ sure        _____ probably not        _____ not sure

**Explain your response.**

**Pray Together:** Thank God for bringing you together. Ask him to bring strength and unity to this marriage.

# Session 3

# One + One = One

**Session 3**

# One + One = One

*The man said, "This is now bone of my bones, and flesh of my flesh; she shall be called woman, because she was taken out of man." For this reason a man shall leave his father and mother, and be joined to his wife; and they shall become one flesh.*
(Genesis 2:23-24)

**What does a man and a woman becoming "one" mean to you?**

**Are there evidences of a oneness already developing in your relationship with your fiancé/fiancée?**

_____ yes _____ no _____ sort of

**Explain your answer.**

## 1. God's Great Math

The non-spiritual person will have trouble understanding God's math when it comes to marriage. How can one plus one equal one (1+1=1) in a marital relationship? Truly the kind of oneness the Bible talks about is a mystery that only can come through a supernatural union done by God himself.

**What does the world do with God's math?**

In the wrestling to make God's mathematics work, the non-spiritual person may try to change the equation.

a. It makes more reasonable sense to say ½ plus ½ equals one. Some see marriage as a union that *completes* a person: A girl becomes a woman, a boy becomes a man. (In Ireland a male is not called a man until he is married or owns property.)

Couples can come into marriage looking for that union to fulfill their dreams. They could find themselves looking to their spouse to fulfill all their needs. Is that God's intention?

* * *

A young woman came to me desperate to be married. She said she was so lonely. She feared being "an old maid." I told her not to get married to fill that need of loneliness. She needed to get close to the one (Jesus Christ) who would meet that need first, then look for a man to marry. She ignored that counsel, married an on-the-road truck driver and now is despairing in depression.

* * *

While God will bring great pleasure and satisfaction to us in the marriage union, it is not his desire that we find wholeness there. We find our wholeness in Christ. Many couples become deeply frustrated — even angry — that their needs and expectations are not fulfilled by their spouse and the marriage deteriorates into a painful relationship of despair.

Jesus Christ is our joy, our peace, our strength… our source of perfect love. When we find our wholeness in him we do not approach marriage as two "halves" seeking to become a whole.

**What needs are you looking to your fiancé/fiancée to meet in your life?**

b. If the quotation is not ½ plus ½ equals one, then perhaps it should rightly be just as we learned in first grade: one plus one equals two (1+1=2). (Obviously God learned his marital math some other place than our first grade classroom.)

Modern culture cries out to couples to deny the true oneness God desires. Many feel pressure to retain his or her own identity, with individual priorities and possessions. For many couples, he is doing *his* thing and she is doing *hers*. They continue to have separate bank accounts, activities, and friends. Some even refuse to take a common name, resisting true oneness, proclaiming that one and one have become *two* united together.

While the oneness of marriage does retain our unique identity, it also transforms every aspect of our identity because of God's supernatural union. Passionately pursuing God's oneness, the words "I," "me," and "mine" begin to vanish from our vocabularies and are replaced by "we," "us," and "ours." The non-spiritual person often resists this oneness, striving to make God's equation to fit one plus one equals two.

**Have you experienced pressure to avoid full oneness in your marriage?**

\_\_\_ yes \_\_\_ no \_\_\_ some

**Explain.**

## 2. True Oneness Accomplished

How does a couple come to realize God's full unity for their marriage? Let's consider four areas in which God desires oneness for you.

a. Spirituality:

> *"I came that they might have life, and might have it abundantly."*
> (John 10:10)

> *"And in him you have been made complete, and he is the head over all rule and authority."*
> (Colossians 2:10)

The only way you can come to the altar and experience the truth of one plus one equals one is that you find yourself now complete in

Christ. If you are looking to your spouse to fill your needs ($\frac{1}{2} + \frac{1}{2} = 1$), you will enter the marriage seeking to take, not give.

If you come into the marriage demanding your rights and the retention of your own distinct identity ($1 + 1 = 2$), your marriage will be full of conflict.

It is only when two people come together who have surrendered to the Lord Jesus Christ, and allowed him to impart his life to them that they can know the oneness in marriage.

**Are you confident that each of you is fully surrendered to Jesus Christ, and that you have found your wholeness in him?**

       \_\_\_ yes     \_\_\_ no     \_\_\_ unsure

**Explain your answer.**

b. Physically

> *"The wife does not have authority over her own body, but the husband does; and likewise also the husband does not have authority over his own body, but the wife does."*
> (1 Corinthians 7:4)

We will spend a whole session discussing the physical aspect of your relationship. For now, it is enough to say that God's oneness can only be accomplished when you come to the realization that marriage means your body is not your own. You now belong to each other. In marriage there is a mutual, intimate sharing of each other to express love and affection.

**What does 1 Corinthians 7:4 mean to you?**

c. Philosophically

> *"Do two men walk together unless they have made an appointment?"*
> (Amos 3:3)

While it is not necessary to agree at every point philosophically, major areas of disagreement will cause strife down the road. Because of your intense emotion now, philosophical differences may seem insignificant but when the flames of passion waiver, the fires of conflict will flare.

Philosophical differences can include political differences such as liberal or conservative. You may have significant differences over how to raise children. Often I see one parent who is very lenient while the other is very strict, creating children who are confused and caught in a crossfire. One couple I knew divorced over the issue of adoption. They learned they could not have children. Philosophically he could not embrace adoption, while she was confident she could love the child as her own. Philosophical differences may not seem significant now but they can become major hurdles in your relationship.

### Philosophical Check List
Circle the answer closest to your opinion.

1. Politically I am:

        liberal    conservative    moderate

2. When it comes to spending I am:

        frugal    carefree    balanced

3. My idea of a good time is:

        staying home    dancing    a movie

4. When a child disobeys, it's time to:

        talk    spank    ignore

5. If we can't have children:

        we won't    we'll adopt    we'll implant

6. When it comes to children, we'll have:

        none    one    two    three    more

7. The house shall be led:
     by the husband    equally both    whoever is strongest

8. Our children will be educated in:
     public school    private school    home school

9. Abortion is:
     wrong    a woman's right    an alternative

10. Homosexuality is:
     a sin    an acceptable alternative    none of my business

**To what degree are you in philosophical agreement?**
(Rate 1 to 10, 10 being best)
0   1   2   3   4   5   6   7   8   9   10

**Explain.**

d. Practically

> *For this reason a man shall leave his father and mother, and be joined to his wife….*
> (Genesis 2:24)

In every way that you can, become practically one. Own all things in common. Avoid having his or her items (other than appropriate items like underwear, toothbrushes, and razors). Something very beautiful happened after our wedding when Elaine sold *her* car, I sold *my* car, and we bought *our* car.

Practical oneness also relates to your relatives. Be careful to respect your parents but not to let them hinder your oneness. I have seen many marriages destroyed by the inability to "leave" Mom and Dad, as the scripture says and cleave to the one God has given to you.

\* \* \*

Martha and Frank had been married about a month. They were definitely still in the honeymoon phase of their marriage. As a wedding gift Martha's parents had given the couple one year's free rent in one of their rental houses. One summer evening as Frank and Martha were watching a movie in their living room, they began to kiss passionately. Suddenly they were aware that someone was standing at the back of the couch. It was Martha's parents. Because they owned the home they felt at liberty to enter without knocking.

\* \* \*

If you think parental influences may present a problem for you and your fiancé/fiancée, I suggest you read *Boundaries* by Henry Cloud and John Townsend.

**Are there any practical hindrances that may stand in the way of your oneness?**

___ yes      ___ no      ___ uncertain

**Explain.**

**Are there any of these four areas where you see potential for concern in your marriage?**

___ spiritually ___ physically ___ philosophically ___ practicality

**Discuss your answer.**

Yes, God's plan for you is one plus one equals one (1+1=1). What an awesome, joyous married life you will find as you pursue the divine oneness God desires for you.

**Prayer Together:** Ask God to reveal how he will work his purposes in your differences. Call upon him to build unity.

# Session 4

# The Unique Assignment

**Session 4**

# The Unique Assignment

*** PLEASE NOTE ***

Prior to reading and completing this session, you should read Ephesians 5:18-33.

> *"Nevertheless, let each individual among you also love his own wife even as himself, and the wife must see to it that she respects her husband."*
> (Ephesians 5:33)

As you enter into marriage, God's word gives a few key points as to your unique role in this relationship. While you hold some marital assignments in common, there are several responsibilities unique to the wife and unique to the husband.

**What are some unique assignments you think may be ahead for you in this marriage?**

The Hebrew custom to help remember a valuable truth was to write the main points in an acrostic. In other words, the first letter of each main point spelled out a key word that brought the truths to mind. In our discussion of your unique roles, as husband and wife, we shall consider "R.E.S.P.E.C.T." for the wife and "C.H.E.R.I.S.H." for the husband. Ladies first.

## 1. R.E.S.P.E.C.T. Your Husband

The "R" is for respect. Since the scripture emphatically says, "see to it" that the wife respects her husband, then we better call attention to it. *Never* demean your husband. Treat him with honor. There may be times you feel he does not deserve your respect but the Bible does not say to respect him when you feel he deserves it. Even in disagreement, show respect.

**Do you respect your fiancé?**

**Explain.**

The "E" is for encouragement. Encouragement is a real need of your husband. Woman was made from man's rib, the bone that guards his heart. You have a ministry of guarding your husband's heart with words of encouragement. Throughout his day he may receive criticism but he needs encouraging words when he comes home to you.

**Do you find it easy to say encouraging words to your fiancé?**

**Explain.**

"S" is for submission which is often misunderstood and resisted. First of all, the scriptures teach that both of you are to mutually submit to one another in the fear of Christ (Ephesians 5:21). The wife, however, is told to submit to her husband. That means to let him lead. He is the head of the home, receiving your counsel, but ultimately responsible to lead.

**What does submission mean to you?**

"P" is for pray. Pray for your husband daily. Pray with your husband, verbally thanking God for him as you hold his hand. Pray for wisdom and strength. Bring specific concerns that face your husband to God in prayer.

**Do you pray regularly for your fiancé?**

**Explain.**

"E" is for exemplify. Exemplify Christ before your husband. Let him see Jesus in you. A powerful verse in 1 Peter reminds us that your example will speak louder to your husband than any words: "In the same way, you wives, be submissive to your own husbands so that even if any of them are disobedient to the word, they may be won without a word by the behavior of their wives" (1 Peter 3:1).

**To what degree do you think you can live by 1 Peter 3:1?**

| 1 | 2 | 3 | 4 | 5 | 6 | 7 | 8 | 9 | 10 |
|---|---|---|---|---|---|---|---|---|---|
| no way | | | | I'll try | | | | you bet! | |

"C" is for counsel. In Genesis 2:18 God said, "It is not good for man to be alone; I will make him a helper suitable for him." The word "helper" in Genesis is the same word used to describe the Holy Spirit in John 14:16. As the Holy Spirit gives counsel and direction, so a wife does for her husband. When you give counsel, don't nag. Give your husband time to consider, and God room to work, for your husband to make decisions.

**How can you help your husband as counselor?**

"T" stands for trust. Trust reflects respect. Trusting your husband's decisions confirms to him your respect. It is difficult at times when you have given counsel to allow him to take another course, demonstrating respect for his judgment.

Trusting his relationships with other women also reveals respect. Women who are extremely jealous and possessive do not respect their husband's integrity or judgment. (I do appreciate the times my wife has said, "I trust you completely, Daryl — but I don't trust her." God has worked through my wife as a warning signal.)

**To what degree do you trust your fiancé?**

| 0 | 1 | 2 | 3 | 4 | 5 | 6 | 7 | 8 | 9 | 10 |
|---|---|---|---|---|---|---|---|---|---|---|
| none | | | | | | | | | | totally |

**Explain.**

**Of your God-given responsibilities (R.E.S.P.E.C.T.), which do you think you may find most difficult to do?**

**Explain.**

## 2. C.H.E.R.I.S.H. Your Wife

The "C" reminds us of the Christlike love you give to your wife. Ephesians 5:25 says to love your wife just as Christ loves the church. He died for us, didn't he? Not only must the husband be willing to die for his wife, he must be willing to live for her. Christlike love is sacrificial. Put her needs ahead of your own.

**Give an example of sacrificially loving your wife.**

"H" is to honor her. She is your bride… your queen. Never speak words that would harm her or demean her. Often in courtship a man will open the door for his lady and show other expressions of polite honor. Too often, however, after the marriage she gets the door herself and he belches and pushes away from the table leaving the cleanup to her after a meal. Always honor her.

**Tell of ways you can honor your bride.**

"E" stands for encouragement. Encouragement must come to the wife from the husband. In many instances where a woman is a stay-at-home mom with small children, she never hears an encouraging word throughout her day.

**Do you find it easy to give encouraging words to your fiancée?**

**Explain.**

"R" stands for refresh. Refresh her. The husband is called the "groom." He has a ministry of grooming his wife to make her more radiant each day. Provide your wife times to rest and be refreshed. Refresh her with the word of God. Ephesians 5:26 is a "grooming" picture: "that he might sanctify her, having cleansed her by the washing of water with the word." Speak God's word over her to bring refreshment to her.

\* \* \*

Bill and Ruth had always had a good marriage, but God blessed them with a new dimension of marriage when Bill began to refresh Ruth with God's word. It began one night when Bill read Psalm 23 personalizing it with Ruth's name. "The Lord is Ruth's shepherd, she shall not want…." He would remind her regularly of who she was in Christ and the promises that were hers to claim. Truly he refreshed her with the word.

* * *

**Give an example of encouraging your fiancée with the word.**

"I" is for intercession. Intercession is an important ministry of the husband. Intercession is praying in your wife's behalf as her advocate. Regularly pray for protection and strength for your wife.

**Do you pray regularly for your fiancée?**

**Explain.**

"S" stands for servant. Be a servant. Jesus was a king… and he was a servant. Even though you are the head of this relationship, you are also the servant. Look for opportunities to serve your wife. Don't put off fixing things that she needs repaired. Pick up your own dirty clothes and help with chores around the house.

**List at least five ways you can serve your wife.**

The "H" is for husband. Be a husband for her. The word "husband" is made up of two words: "house" and "band." A house-band protects and provides security for his wife. He protects her from physical distress, emotional hardships, and spiritual attacks. Be alert to forces that would come against your wife and do what you can with God's help to defend her.

**How can you protect your bride spiritually?**

**Of your God-given responsibilities (C.H.E.R.I.S.H.), which do you think you may find most difficult to do?**

**Explain your answer.**

### 3. Not On Your Own

What you are given to do, you cannot do in your own strength. You need God's help. You need his grace and power by the Holy Spirit working in you and through you. Ask God to help you be the marriage partner He has called you to be.

*I can do all things through him who strengthens me.*
(Philippians 4:13)

**Pray Together:** Take time for each of you to ask God to help you fulfill your role in this marriage. Thank him for each other.

# Session 5

# Financial Feuds
# Can Fuel Failure

**Session 5**

# Financial Feuds Can Fuel Failure

*For the love of money is a root of all sorts of evil, and some by longing for it have wandered away from the faith and pierced themselves with many griefs. But flee from these things, you man of God, and pursue righteousness, godliness, faith, love, perseverance, and gentleness.*
(1 Timothy 6:10-11)

The majority of divorced couples will tell you that financial problems were at least a part of the cause for their marital failure. It is so easy to become consumed with money matters. Blame is a typical response when ends are not meeting. All of these financial pitfalls can be avoided if you lay a firm biblical foundation for how your finances will be handled.

Approximately how much do you think you will spend monthly in each of the following areas (be sure to do this work on your own):

ITEM                                              MONTHLY EXPENSE

Food                                                    _____
Rent / House Payment                                    _____
Utilities (include phone)                               _____
Clothing                                                _____
Church & other charitable gifts                         _____
Insurance: Car / Health / Life / Home                   _____
Entertainment - Movies, Concerts, Meals Out, and so on  _____

Will you use a credit card?                 ___ yes ___ no ___ ?
Will you borrow to buy a car?               ___ yes ___ no ___ ?
Will you borrow to buy a home?              ___ yes ___ no ___ ?
Will you begin to save now for the future?  ___ yes ___ no ___ ?
Will all monies be in joint accounts?       ___ yes ___ no ___ ?

**To what degree are you in agreement on financial matters?**
(Circle the number that best represents your agreement)

| 0 | 1 | 2 | 3 | 4 | 5 | 6 | 7 | 8 | 9 | 10 |
|---|---|---|---|---|---|---|---|---|---|---|
| not at all | | | | pretty good | | | | | we agree! | |

**Explain.**

As you begin your married life together, the financial decisions you make *now* will have an influence on your future. Lay a firm foundation based on biblical principles. Here are ten financial tips to consider as you move into marriage.

1. Set up a budget and use it. Make sure your budget is "do-able" and practical. Work to create a budget in agreement, not with one of you dictating terms to the other. Crown Financial Ministries has excellent tools for helping you develop a workable budget and staying on it (www.crown.org). Too often couples develop a budget then ignore it. Live by your budget. Be good stewards (Genesis 1:28).

**Are you committed to making a budget and living by it?**

**Explain.**

2. Avoid trying to keep up with others, family, friends, or neighbors, striving to have what they have. There is much pressure to have the newest car, the nicest house, the best furniture, the latest entertainment center. Don't short circuit your financial stability trying to satisfy an appetite to have what others have. Avoid a heart of coveting (Exodus 17:20).

**To what degree do you struggle with wanting what others have?**

| 1 | 2 | 3 | 4 | 5 | 6 | 7 | 8 | 9 | 10 |
|---|---|---|---|---|---|---|---|---|---|
| I don't struggle | | | | | | | it's a real problem | | |

**Explain.**

3. Plan ahead for large expenditures. The paper is full of ads in December and January of loan offices wanting to "help" you with Christmas expenses. If you had set aside $50 per month, you would have been ready for Christmas. I am amazed at how many panic when the insurance premium or property taxes come due, as if they forgot that payment was going to be required. Lay back money monthly for those large expenditures (Proverbs 6:6).

**Will you plan ahead for those big expenditures?**

**Explain.**

4. You can even plan ahead for crises. Your car will break down. Things in your home will break, needing repair or replacement. Lay-off is always a possibility. While we cannot foresee every crisis, the wise steward lays back a resource for what might come. Because we set aside $50 per month for car repairs, we were able to write out a check for an expensive brake job our car needed recently (Proverbs 6:6).

**What is the advantage of planning for crises?**

5. Do not exceed your budget. Do not spend money you do not have. I have counseled with couples who have thousands of dollars charged on credit cards who have dug themselves into a hopeless hole of debt. If the money is not there to spend now, do not spend what you *hope* to make tomorrow. It is tough to tell yourself "no," but the pain of debt will be avoided for the future (Romans 13:8). If you have serious debt issues currently, seek financial counsel to resolve these matters prior to your wedding.

**What is your attitude about debt?**

6. Use credit cards wisely. If you cannot exercise wisdom and self-control in the use of a credit card, don't use a credit card at all. Your goal should be to pay the balance in full, never paying any interest. Look for a card that has no annual fee.

\* \* \*

We use a credit card that has no annual fee and pays a percentage per purchase. Each time we use the credit card we record it in our checkbook and subtract it from our balance just as if we had written a check. When I pay the credit card bill, I have nothing to subtract, pay no interest, and receive a monthly bonus. Last year we received a check for nearly $200 for using our credit card.

\* \* \*

Remember — a credit card is not the problem. The one holding it is (1 Timothy 6:10-11).

**Are credit cards a problem for you?**

**Have they been in the past?**

**Explain your responses.**

7. Shop wisely. Watch for sales. As a rule, you can manage to purchase most items at some discount. Do your homework well when purchasing a large item. Consult *Consumer Reports* as to value and quality. Remember, cheapest is not always best. Quality matters too. Do not be afraid to buy used items. The greatest mark-up is on items that are new (Luke 16:8).

**Are you willing to buy used items?**

**Explain.**

8. Prioritize your spending according to biblical guidelines. Prayerfully discern your needs ahead of your wants. Guard your hearts of greed, covetedness, or self-reliance. Invite the Holy Spirit to work in your budgeting process (Matthew 6:33).

**What are the top three priorities of your budget?**

9. Are there any destructive habits that are robbing you financially? Habits such as gambling, drug addiction, alcohol use, cigarette smoking, or pornography can erode one's financial stability. I have seen people sacrifice having adequate nourishment in order to have cigarettes or beer. Prayerfully evaluate your expenses to see if any of your resources are being invested in things that are unnecessary and even harmful (John 10:10a).

**Are there any destructive habits that will rob you in your finances?**

**Explain.**

10. Be givers. "Now this I say, he who sows sparingly will also reap sparingly, and he who sows bountifully will also reap bountifully. Each one must do just as he has purposed in his heart, not grudgingly or under compulsion, for God loves a cheerful giver" (2 Corinthians 9:6-7).

In our budget, the tithe (10% to God's work) and offerings (gifts above the tithe) are a top priority. If we put God and his kingdom first, the rest will fall into place (Matthew 6:33).

The prophet Malachi wrote about tithing, "Bring the whole tithe into the storehouse, so that there may be food in my house, and test me now in this," says the Lord of hosts, "if I will not open for you the windows of heaven and pour out for you a blessing until it overflows" (Malachi 3:10).

Remember all that we have really belongs to God, so be generous to use your resources for God's purposes.

**Are you committed to tithing?**

**Explain.**

**Review the ten tips.**

**Which three do you consider to be most important?**

**Which tips do you think may be the most difficult for you and your fiancé/fiancée?**

The responsible use of finances is a crucial ingredient to a happy home. Take seriously the encouragement to get on a budget and live on that budget. In the years to come, you will be grateful you did.

**Pray Together:** Thank God for how he has provided for you. Ask him to guide you to be good stewards of your finances.

# Session 6

# My Body
# Is Not My Own

**Session 6**

# My Body Is Not My Own

*The husband must fulfill his duty to his wife, and likewise also the wife to her husband. The wife does not have authority over her own body, but the husband does; and likewise also the husband does not have authority over his own body, but the wife does.*
(1 Corinthians 7:3-4)

**What do the verses from 1 Corinthians 7 say to *you*?**

It was a popular sitcom, but it was a scene you could have seen in many sitcoms — or in too many homes. The couple has had an argument. The wife stomps into the bedroom grabs a pillow and blanket, throws them in her husband's face, and says, "You're sleeping on the couch." In other words, until this matter is settled to the wife's satisfaction, there will be no sexual relations.

Sex is abused and misused in many marriages. It is a beautiful gift of God to be mutually shared and enjoyed throughout your lifetime. God's word has some very practical things to say about your sexual relationship.

## 1. Your Body Is Not Your Own
## (1 Corinthians 7:3-4)

Part of the oneness you will experience as husband and wife will be sexual intercourse. The biblical view is one of "my body no longer is mine… it is his… or hers." You will belong to each other. Therefore you have relinquished personal rights in good faith, trust, love, and devotion to each other.

What does it mean to relinquish rights? First of all, it by no means gives way to an abusive situation. It means that both of you have hearts set on pleasing your spouse physically, never *using* sex to punish or control the other. The key to the success of this biblical picture is that both of you understand the concept. Paul is telling us that the sexual relationship is *not* 50%-50% — it is *not* give and take. It is 100% give — from *both* of you, then you will find great delight.

**Do you think you will be willing to fully give yourself to your spouse?**

_____ yes       _____ no       _____ unsure

**Explain.**

## 2. Mutual Consent Is God's Design

Before you begin to think that giving yourself fully to your spouse means that you must have sex at any time or place he or she demands, we must read on to verse 5 of 1 Corinthians 7: "Stop depriving one another, except by agreement for a time, so that you may devote yourselves to prayer, and come together again so that Satan will not tempt you because of your lack of self-control."

The overall scriptural concept of the sexual relationship is one of mutuality. Because you both have fully, mutually relinquished your rights to the other, you are in a relationship of giving yourself to your spouse. Out of that mutual love and sharing, there are also times you will agree together to abstain from sexual intercourse.

Two biblical principles are clear from Paul's words:

**a. Abstaining needs to be done with agreement.**
The foundational truth to remember here is that *the decision to have or to not have sex should never be made by one member of the relationship alone*. It should always be a *mutual* decision.

Paul speaks of prayer as one reason for mutually abstaining. There are, however, other legitimate reasons for the couple to agree to refrain from sexual intercourse. Sickness, late-term pregnancy, fatigue, stress, conflict, all can be justifiable reasons to abstain. The important matter is to talk — and come to a place of mutual agreement.

**Why is mutual agreement so important when it comes to the decision to refrain from sexual intercourse?**

**b. It is not good to abstain too long.**
Paul warns not to stay apart too long, or you will give the devil an opportunity to tempt you. Don't be fooled by the cunning enemy, thinking you can go for long periods of time without sexual relations. Even though it may not lead to unfaithfulness, it will diminish the richness of your union and allow the enemy, and your flesh, to direct your thought-life into forbidden territory.

**Give five good reasons to make your times of sexual abstinence as brief as possible.**

### 3. Understanding Leads to Delight

When it comes to sexual activity, men and women are very different. Through dialogue (and perhaps some study) it is valuable to understand those differences and grow with them. Francis of Assisi taught us a tremendous prayer that encourages us to be people more set on understanding others rather than being understood. Strive to understand how the two of you differ regarding sex. Here are some helpful hints to remember.

**a. Men and women view sex differently.**
When asked why they participated in sexual intercourse before marriage, men answered, "Because I love *it*." Women answered, "Because I love *him*." Among men, *Playboy* is the number-one best seller. Women hold *Better Homes and Gardens* as their favorite. Men tend to view sex as an event or activity, while women see sex as a relational experience of intimacy.

**b. Men and women approach sex differently.**
Someone once said that when it comes to sex, women are like crock pots, and men are like microwave ovens. Men, being primarily visually stimulated, tend to be ready for sexual intercourse quickly while women are still thinking about the book they had been reading. A woman needs her husband to take his time and to assure her that his love is for *her*, not for *sex*.

**c. Men and women conclude sex differently.**
Microwaves not only heat up quickly, they finish the job fast as well. Often after climax a man is done, ready to roll over, and go to sleep. The woman is still very much sexually and *emotionally* energized. She is delighted with caressing and kissing even after climax.

As you both are sensitive to these differences and communicate with one another, you will see your sex life get more precious with each passing day of marriage.

**What are some other differences you can think of in how men and women approach sexual activity?**


## 4. Communication Is Crucial for Sexual Fulfillment

Be willing to discuss sexual matters with your spouse. Sex is not a forbidden topic and discussion about sexual intercourse will not diminish the satisfaction you both will find… it will enhance it.

\* \* \*

Chuck and Mary remained married for less than two years. Their sexual relationship had never been fulfilling. Unknown to Chuck, sexual intercourse was very painful for Mary, and because of that she avoided sex, coming up with excuses to refrain. Chuck experienced constant rejection and hurt. He tried to get Mary to talk about their sexual problems, even encouraging counseling. Mary grew up with the conviction that sex was a forbidden topic of discussion.

She refused to discuss or seek counsel for their problems. A few months after their divorce, Mary learned she had a birth defect which restricted her sexual activity, making intercourse difficult and painful. Sadly, too late she learned a truth that could have brought help to their marriage. Her unwillingness to talk or seek counsel led to the end of her marriage.

* * *

Always be willing to discuss sexual matters. There are a few questions I encourage couples to discuss often:

1. Ask your spouse if there is anything in your sexual activity that makes them uncomfortable or feel demeaned. Listen non-defensively to their reply.

2. Talk about ways to improve your sexual relationship. Ask your spouse if there are things you can do to make the sexual encounter more meaningful.

3. Be certain that emotionally you are in a good place before the physical activity begins. Ask if there is some offense, hurt, or anger that is unresolved.

Communicate your love and devotion to one another daily, throughout the day. Speak words of encouragement and praise to your spouse that genuinely communicates your love for him or her as a person.

**To what degree do you feel comfortable to talk about sex with your fiancé/fiancée?**

0    1    2    3    4    5    6    7    8    9    10
not at all                  mostly                     very

**Explain.**

## 5. Keep the Marriage Bed Pure!

Paul wrote to the Corinthians, "For you have been bought with a price: therefore glorify God in your body" (1 Corinthians 6:20). Remember that your body... your sexual relationship... your whole marriage belongs to God and is to be an avenue for God to be glorified.

The author of Hebrews wrote, "Marriage is to be held in honor among all, and the marriage bed is to be undefiled; for fornicators and adulterers God will judge" (Hebrews 13:4).

Keep your relationship pure in the sight of God and each other. Stay absolutely faithful to your spouse, not looking to the left or to the right with desire for another.

Avoid pornographic materials. Find your sexual stimulation only in your spouse. It is an offense to your wife or husband that you require looking upon another woman or man to find sexual satisfaction.

Avoid sexual jokes that demean God's gift of sex and make sexual intercourse out to be something dirty or obscene.

**Can you think of other attitudes or activities that might defile your marriage bed?**

Your sexual relationship is a wonderful gift from God. Work together to make it more precious all of your days together on planet earth.

An excellent resource on the topic of sexual fulfillment is Dr. Ed Wheat's book, *Intended for Pleasure*.

If you have questions or concerns about your sexual relationship, find a trusted Christian friend or counselor and discuss those issues *before* marriage.

**Pray Together:** Thank God for the gift of sexual intimacy. Ask him to bless your union.

# Session 7

# The 3-D/3-C Marriage

# The 3-D/3-C Marriage

*"And be subject to one another in the fear of Christ."*
(Ephesians 5:21)

In this final session, you will consider three dimensions of a marriage. **WARNING: If any one of these dimensions is neglected, your marriage will fail.** It may not mean you end up in divorce, but it will certainly mean the marriage will not be all God intended for you.

Imagine that the three dimensions of marriage form a triangle. Pull any side out and the triangle will collapse. This 3-D triangle is actually made up of 3-C's… Christ, communication, and commitment.

**1. The first dimension is Christ.** He is the foundation. If Christ is not at the center of this marriage, your union will fail to be all that God wants it to be. Jesus Christ must be the integral part of your relationship.

The author of Hebrews encouraged us to fix our eyes on Jesus, the author and perfecter of our faith. As you fix your eyes on Jesus, seeking to please him, seeking to be like him, your marriage will find great fulfillment.

Colossians 3:17 says, "Whatever you do in word or deed, do all in the name of the Lord Jesus." That means your words and actions should be representative of Jesus Christ. Treat your spouse as Christ would. Say to your spouse what Jesus would say. Would Jesus call him stupid? Would Jesus treat her like a slave?

Colossians 3:23 says, "Whatever you do, do your work heartily, as for the Lord." That means to respond to your spouse as you would respond to Jesus. Treat them the way you would treat Jesus — with respect, devotion, and love.

Can you see how marriages would be transformed if: 1) We would treat each other the way Christ would? and 2) We would treat each other the way we would treat Christ? That is precisely what a Christ-centered marriage would reflect.

**Give examples of...**
**Treating your spouse the way Christ would treat him/her.**

**Treating your spouse as you would treat Christ Jesus himself.**

**Is Jesus at the center of your relationship?**
            ___ yes      ___ no      ___ unsure

**Explain.**

Having Christ as head of your marriage will be reflected concretely in your home life. He will influence every aspect of your life.

* * *

One time a couple was answering questions in a premarital counseling session regarding spiritual matters. When asked if they prayed together they said, "No." When asked if they attended church and if they had discussed plans about church after marriage they said, "No." The question was asked if they thought the Bible would be an influence in their home, one said "No" and the other said "Uncertain." Even after all that, when asked if Christ were the center of the relationship, they both answered "Yes." Was he really?

* * *

While spiritual activity is not an absolute measure of spirituality, inactivity can be a warning flag as to the role Christ will have in the new home being established.

**Are you spiritually active together?**

**Explain.**

**2. A second dimension your marriage must have is communication.**

**How would you measure your communication skills?**
(Circle the number closest to your rating.)

| 0 | 1 | 2 | 3 | 4 | 5 | 6 | 7 | 8 | 9 | 10 |
|---|---|---|---|---|---|---|---|---|---|---|
| poor | | so-so | | fair | | good | | | excellent | |

**Explain.**

**Now rate your fiancé/fiancée.**

| 0 | 1 | 2 | 3 | 4 | 5 | 6 | 7 | 8 | 9 | 10 |
|---|---|---|---|---|---|---|---|---|---|---|
| poor | | so-so | | fair | | good | | | excellent | |

**Explain.**

Communication is talking and listening. It is using words wisely and respectfully.

Communication is expressing not only information, but emotions.

Most couples who have divorced list as the primary factor of the demise of their marriage the breakdown of communication.

Set aside daily time to communicate. Ask each other meaningful questions about life. Talk about activities, dreams, and fears.

Communicate often of your love for your spouse. The words "I love you" (and other words of affection) add fuel to the fires of your love for one another.

Communication is like a garden. It must be well-tended. Keep weeds of bitterness and suspicion from gaining root by openly discussing your feelings. Water the good crops with caring questions and careful listening. Till the soil by talking frequently, keeping it tilled by deep conversations of meaningful topics. Too often I've seen the garden of communication well-tended in the early years of marriage, only to fall into tangled fruitlessness by neglect in the latter years.

Elaine and I found that if you allow it to happen, children can be a barrier in your communication. Someone once said that once you have children you must surrender ever finishing a thought — or a sentence. You must work harder at communication once you have children. Be sure to schedule regular "dates." We have overnights away from the children that are for both planning and playing. When I come home from work I seek out Elaine first, not the children, and we take a few moments to review our day. We work at keeping the communication channels clear and active.

* * *

If at any time your spouse feels the need to seek counsel, feeling there is a breakdown of communication, resolve and pledge right now that you will be willing to participate.

_____ I pledge to be willing to seek counsel at any time my spouse feels it is necessary.

Signed: _____

* * *

**What are some things you can do to keep communication lines open?**

**3. The third dimension of the marriage that must not be neglected is commitment!**

Several years ago a young couple came to their pastor to get married. They asked him if they could change the vows. The pastor was surprised and puzzled and said, "How do you want to change the vows?" They answered, "We want to say, 'as long as we both shall love' instead of as long as we both shall live." The pastor would not agree to their request.

The couple wanted to base their marriage on emotion rather than on devotion. There may be times you do not feel like you love each other but your commitment must carry you through those times.

On your wedding day you will stand before God and family and friends and make very serious vows. You will promise to stay with your spouse until *death* separates you. Do you take those vows seriously?

On your wedding day you will say, "I'll stay for better or for worse." How worse is "worse"? Most couples do fine on the "better" part, but when the "worse" part comes, many part.

You will also say, "In sickness and in health."

Ron came back from the war shell-shocked. He was mentally incompetent. He had to be placed in an institution. Mary was encouraged to divorce him. Her friends told her that she deserved a life, and that Ron could never be a real husband for her. She replied, "I promised that in sickness and in health, I would never leave him." What rare devotion!

You will say, "For richer or for poorer." As you read earlier, many divorced people list financial matters as the source of their conflict. Many times a divorce follows bankruptcy or job loss. Separations have also come after great financial gain.

**Are you committed to your fiancé/fiancée and to the vows you will make to one another?**

**What would you consider to be grounds for divorce?**

Jesus had a perspective on divorce quite different from those around him.

*Getting up, He went from there to the region of Judea and beyond the Jordan; crowds gathered around him again, and, according to his custom, he once more began to teach them. Some Pharisees came up to Jesus, testing him, and began to question him whether it was lawful for a man to divorce a wife.*

*And he answered and said to them, "What did Moses command you?"*

*They said, "Moses permitted a man to write a certificate of divorce and send her away."*

*But Jesus said to them, "Because of your hardness of heart he wrote you this commandment. But from the beginning of creation, God made them male and female. For this reason a man shall leave his father and mother, and the two shall become one flesh; so they are not longer two, but one flesh. What therefore God has joined together, let no man separate."*
(Mark 10:1-9)

As was his custom, Jesus often changed the focus of the question. While the Pharisees asked about divorce, Jesus turned the focus on marriage. He pointed out to them that marriage was something God did, concluding with the words, "What therefore God has joined together, let no man separate."

Perhaps even in our culture, the cause for so much divorce is that we don't grasp the covenantal commitment of marriage. It is a union established by God for a lifetime. That's why we must have God's guidance at the beginning of the relationship, and his strength and help throughout all the days we share together. Let me assure you — God is committed to the success of your marriage. May he grant you a willingness to be as committed as well.

# For Review

What are the three C's of a 3-D relationship.

C_____              C_____

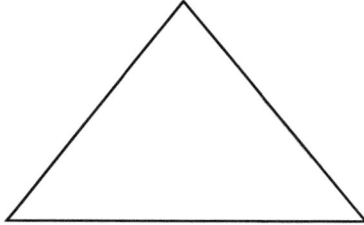

C_____

Are you committed to be attentive to maintain health in each of the three aspects of your marriage?

_____ I am        _____ I think so        _____ no

**Pray Together:** Thank God for the commitment you have made to each other. Surrender totally to Christ. Thank him for bringing you together.

# Addendum

# Marrying Again —
# A Time For Reflection

Addendum

# Marrying Again —
# A Time for Reflection

*"For I hate divorce," says the Lord, the God of Israel, "and him who covers his garment with wrong," says the Lord of hosts. "So take heed to your spirit, that you do not deal treacherously."*
(Malachi 2:16)

Divorce has become far too common in our culture. The prophet Malachi wrote that God hates divorce. He did not write that God hates divorced people. He hates the pain and loss divorce always brings.

Jesus acknowledged that we live in a world where hardness of heart leads to hurt and brokenness. In every divorce, one or both had a hard, unwilling heart to allow God to come in and heal.

I am convinced most divorces stem from the very inception of the relationship. The relationship was not founded in God's will, grounded in his word, nor centered in Christ. (That's precisely why I believe that serious pre-marital preparation is essential.)

The good news is God is the God of new beginnings. He is the supernatural God of impossible odds. I've seen him restore marriages that were considered beyond hope. I've seen him heal and make new individuals who were broken by the pain of divorce.

As you are considering remarriage, please carefully and prayerfully proceed. The decision to remarry is more complicated and serious than even the decision to marry. Take special time with your pastor discussing the biblical perspectives on divorce and remarriage.

Sometime prior to this relationship you are now in, you made vows to another that you would see the marriage through until death separated you. You said, "for better or worse, in sickness and in health, in wealth or poverty," yet for some reason, that covenant has been broken. Let me encourage you, that even if you were not the one who initiated the termination of your first marriage, deeply search your heart regarding your role in the marriage.

Prior to your discussion with your pastor or counselor, candidly fill out the questionnaire on page 81.

# For People
# Who Have Been Divorced

In the event that either of you have been married before, there are some serious issues you must consider:

1. How long have you been divorced?

2. What was the cause of your divorce?

3. Were you unfaithful?

4. Who filed for the divorce?

5. Have you resolved the issues of your previous marriage?

6. What problems might you be bringing into this marriage?

7. Are there unsettled issues regarding children?

8. You said vows of a life commitment to one person. Now you are making them to another. Are you both at peace with those circumstances?

9. Are you absolutely certain your first union is totally over?

10. Have you confessed your failings in the first marriage and asked for God's forgiveness?

11. What gives you new confidence that this marriage will work?

www.ingramcontent.com/pod-product-compliance
Lightning Source LLC
LaVergne TN
LVHW021543080426
835509LV00019B/2817

# In Conclusion

May God bless you as you begin your married life together. Remember, good marriages don't just happen. You must work together at maintaining a strong union, with Christ at the center.

Attend a vibrant, biblical church together where you will find encouragement, prayer, and counsel. Look to your pastor and other mature Christians to help you stay on track.

Make the commitment to participate in marital enrichment events. Your pastor can help you make arrangements.

Keep growing and glowing in the love that brought you together.